Weird Pl....
poems and lyrics

WEIRD PLEASURE

POEMS AND LYRICS

JIM FERGUSON
LEAMINGTON BOOKS

Weird Pleasure
Jim Ferguson

All rights Jim Ferguson 2021
Published by Leamington Books
32 Leamington Terrace
Edinburgh, Scotland

Set in Bookman Old Style
Printed and bound in The United Kingdom

Cover art by Louise Malone
Layout by German Creative
Set by Peter Burnett

leamingtonbooks.com
ISBN 9780955488535

Contents

breakfast – a sequence about myself

Weird Pleasure

overture

flat-cap man
on St Vincent Street

walks on against
the home from work crowd

tears in his eyes
head tilted forward

trouser pockets
full of fists

old trainers crunch
the ground

inside a doorway
puts his head down

gathers up his knees
like a foetus

song of the nervous breakdown

put your mind in a jar
put your mind in a jar
and
pop it in the cupboard

sky-full of stars
in a tea-spoon of sugar
secrets all sleeping
in a cloud-full of dreams
the past is a wasteland
and the future just an empty scream

screen upon screen
of marketing dreams
juxtaposed
with wall to wall terror
now how on earth-dyou expect
to remain sane in that drain

rapidly algorithms rob all your neighbours
not ever allowed to go slow
trademarks and copyrights on apples and windows
and it's all made of nothing and one, just zero and
    one

sky-full of stories
in a tea-cup in your mind,
crowded with chocolates
all sweet and benign,
and your body's not twitching
as the planets float in a line
—and even when you're random

all your dinner courses always arrive,
the equations have rules just to please you,
and the robots obey,
they will serve you all day
in that restaurant of truth in the sky—

put your mind in a jar
and follow the instructions
pop your mind in a jar
heat it and feel it expand
put your mind jar
feel it shatter when the glass gets too hot

rapidly algorithms rob all your reason
and you're never allowed to go slow
trademarks and copyrights on emotions and
    feelings
and it's all made of nothing and doubt, just
    zero and dark

alex harvey was our guide

this is not radio 4
it's verbal liberation
thundering through your door

this is not radio 3
it's a crazy gladness
flying into your tree

this is not radio 2
it's a sonic transformation
heading straight to you

this is alive, a real living space
this is street-life
it's a jungle full of grace

this is a man with stockings in his mouth
this is writing on our walls
with no need to head south

this is our voice, it's a glaswegian call
they think it's funny when you fuck up
and it's funny when you fall

a cartoon hero with a dignified chant
with a crazy striped shirt
and a beatific rant

this is heh jimmy with a slice of jaques brel
it's a theatre of sound
you can touch, taste and smell

this is life uncovered as your feet take the floor
and your swimming up a river
you did not know you loved before

it's a tree and a fish
it's a bird and a bell
and aw that other crap that the tourist shops sell

it's laughter and hope and depression and death
it's a different holy book
it's your heartbeat and your breath

this is where they rob you
of your skills and your wealth
this is chain smoking life, it's inherent ill health

they will call you a nutter
they will call you off your fucking tree
if never the exploited nor exploiter shall ye be

this is radio without wage slaves
this is radio in your head
this is radio anything that you want to say instead

this is not radio 2
this is not radio 3
this is not radio 4

this is not radio 4
it's a live space
it's a door

it's a wide open door
it's a free and vibrant floor

    this
        is
            not
                radio 4

John Lennon's Elbow Transmits Text Messages to ma Brain

some people live in their cars
they go about with sniper's eyes
keep their guns in sleeping bags
they're real regular guys

some folk live in the stars
shining bright with delusion
got control of their minds right now
but the only way to go is mad

some folk live in shanty towns
electricity's what they lack
they got no water to cook in
got whips biting into their backs

newspapers keep me warm at night
newspapers tell me the truth

ah got a bed of roses
ah got a bed of nails
ah got a bed of concrete and bones
got a sailboat with out any sails

and some folk
they can build their boats
and some folk
they can cook
others can cure cancer
and some folk
they write books
sad bastards — with Mozart ringtones
sit on trains in trances destroying world peace

and
quiet is far too quiet
and
loud is way too loud
and
young is always much too young
and
old is already dead dead old — pure dead but
brilliant old
by the way
and
middle aged is totally fucked

and
everybody's useless
except
mrs greedy and mr lust — the thrusting
entrepreneurs

wah wwwaaaaahhhhhhh
(Scream: WWHHAAAAAAAAHHHH)

ahm oan msn
ahm oan lycos too
ahm oan cable, terrestrial, satellite and the broo
ahm oan dynamite without the mss
ahm oan ec-sta-cy
ahm oan bullets and Trojan horses
ahm oan LSD and GHB and horse pills that
    keep yi gouched
ahm oan Moto sponsored movies
ahm oan Rubik's cube
ahm oan Diners Club and shrapnel
ahm oan change for the bus

ahm away to get a real joab noo
tell yi ma heid's totally fucked

coz

John
    Lennon's
        Elbow
            Transmits
                Text Messages
                    To Ma Brain

weighing water

the weight of water
lies so heavy
no blue soul
can move within
its orbit
all the molecules
are so dense
there's no room
to vibrate
nothing but stasis
ending in
death

*

if you think it's something to be cheerful about
just jump

*

there's not an incredible mind-machine
made of electrical impulses we know of

yet

that isn't just as perishable
as the brain inside your head

*

try out your drinking song
even try drinking
once you're obliterated

20

it all feels the same

so i'm told

*

if you can dance in the rain like gene kelly
you probably aren't mentally ill

but if you dance those steps on a dry day
busy with buzzing shoppers

they will think you're crazy

*

unlike frozen yoghurt
frozen rain is very miserable

as it lashes your face
and your ears sting

because

you have the wrong
kind of hat

so having the wrong kind of hat
is for many

one of the great and grotesque
sources

of misery

*

if you have a serious
nicotine addiction

the best cure
is to sit in a small row-boat

out in the middle
of the atlantic ocean

and wait to see
if anyone comes along

and offers you one last smoke
before you die

*

and you loved in the hedgerow for martyrs
with birds eggs and tropical fish

and when they hosed you down in the
morning
the water it smelt just like piss

and they called for sycophants and siphons
for stanks and for drains and for hydrants

in dreams w—h—e—r—e the malnourished
    may dwell
for you're better off under the hedgerow

than locked up aw by yirsel

*

at standard temperature and pressure
one cubic centimetre of water

is always the same mass
no matter what the government sells

it always hurts your heart
when you're so deep under

no light can intrude
on the dark

but

in the

lightness of water

there are...

...spiders webs and silken threads
drift wood splinters, soapy bubbles
tiny dust specks, hot-air balloons
clouds, light-beams, feathers and sounds

spays and droplets, rain as smirr
paper letters spelling H 2 O
escapes from gravity
wandering thoughts

one-two-three-four
bees go moo and song-birds roar
five-six-seven-eight

so light of head you can't walk straight

nine-ten- eleven-twelve
rainbows casting magic spells
thirteen-fourteen-fifteen-sixteen
and all the fractions in-between

seventeen- eighteen...
no need to go further
cause eighteen
is the weight of water

water comes in molecules
gathers together in puddles and pools
it can be gas or solid or liquid
depending on how hot it is

H_2O

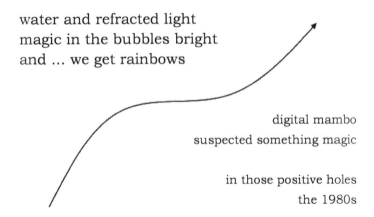

water and refracted light
magic in the bubbles bright
and ... we get rainbows

digital mambo
suspected something magic

in those positive holes
the 1980s

redolent with greed
dancing in the streets of steel towns

all the wreckage tumbling
just before the nano-computer

was sewn in the fabric of your nerve cells

> rapidly algorithms
> rob all your neighbours
> not ever allowed to go slow
> trademarks and copyrights
> on apples and windows
> and it's all made of nothing and one
> just zeros and ones

if your body's too acidic you will die

*

fished out
a dead spider
from the back of the sink
the dodgy bit
no one goes near

it was
a dead
black mambo
digital spider
and the corpse
filled me with fear

footer roon the hoose
wae a wee hat oan ma heid
thirs muckle snaw ootside
am in a dwam aboot whas deid

spiders

the moon's in the sky
and we're under the eaves
transfixed by the fact we're alive

those octagonal beasts
stretch their legs in the gloom
old spiders relaxing
we glimpse them
through fingers
that cover our eyes

something primal
in the way we've evolved
a fear that helps us survive

out of the soup we rose up,
and from our sophisticated whistling-lips
we spout forth mesmeric tunes
to distract us from rage and from doom
we invented the bomb
to blind us from fear

under the moon
transfixed by terror and dread-filled
amazed we were ever alive

Art of Hostile

The government made this land
Hostile to migrants
Hostile to travellers who aren't just tourists
Hostile to youth and to those without phones
Hostile to folk who don't own their own homes
Hostile to languages other than English
Hostile because you can't find the right job
Hostile to those who don't wear the right clothes
Hostile to those who can't walk very far or fast
    down the road
Hostile to those who resist exploitation
Hostile to those who go on strike
Hostile to walking or riding a bike
Though
There's always a welcome for money and cars

But if these prized possessions you are without
The government made this land
An hostile environment
Hostility, passive-aggressive and smart —

The creation of hostile environments
Has become a fine art

fertility

so cold
the sheets of ice
could slit your throat

morning sickness
crawls
inside your guts

you slip
and go on rolling
down the hill

the morning sickness
flies
your baby's dead

in shock
you lie concussed
the cold melts into you

but
you call out for the father
not yourself

you're just not thinking
of
yourself

there's a mouthful sick
by your defeated face
—a circle on the ice

the grace of angels
helpless
to console.

wiseblood

pin-point of light
do you think that it's easter
the angels can't dance for you anymore
they can't dance for you anymore...

pin-point of light
do you think that it's easter
nothing comes back
and no one can help you

in the cold river clyde
where sanity drowned
there's a hole in your head
to let in the sun

pin-point of life
you're a pick and an axe
the tip of a needle
and the angels in boots

can't dance for you anymore
they can't fly for you anymore
feet swollen fat and marble lungs
and the box never floats

it just carries you off
back to atoms and flame
as burst stomachs look on
pus dripping down cheeks

pin-point of light
peeping out your black coat
the pus all pours in
closes everything down

closes it all down forever
closes it all down forever

pin-point of light
do you think that it's easter
the angels can't dance for you anymore
they can't dance for you anymore...

serenade

bored with sex
bored with sex
bored with talking about sex

bored with life
bored with life
bored with talking about life

she screwed you to the floor
left your heart fucked by the door—

and when you're tongue tied
not all peanut butter tastes the same
when your fire's out
and your little plastic lighter has no flame
and when you're broken
looking bored is how to hide your pain

living war
re-living war
when you're home from the war

on the floor
on the floor
crawling underneath the floor

falling fast
gone at last
meeting earth and dust at last—

when you've been dangled far too long
on the end of that rope
the cock-pit has vanished
and the boxing ring's closed
no more punches to throw
no more blues to evade
off to hell in a handcart
with a slow   slow-slow
s e r e n a d e
            s e r e n a d e

we're not supposed to

we're not supposed to
be feral children
happy to wander the streets of our talents

we're not supposed to
walk
on the road where the cars go

we're not supposed to
talk
to the police in the wrong strong tone

we're not supposed to
disrespect
millionaires' private property

we're not supposed to
tune
into the news from Russia Today

we're not supposed to
get
drunk until we're sent to jail

we're not supposed to
take
control of our beautiful souls

we're not supposed to
steal
the wigs from balding judges

we're not supposed to
appear
on *Star Trek The Next Generation* or *Big Bang*

we're not supposed to
outlive
lazy lords who call themselves farmers

we're not supposed to
caress
our lovers with toil-weary hands

we're not supposed to
mark
life in seasons but only in storms

we're not supposed to
forget
to harvest an over-ripe crop

we're not supposed to
neglect
our couscous for tatties and rice

we're not supposed to
eat
excessive amounts of sugar and spice

we're not supposed to
extract
our own teeth with a dentist in sight

we're not supposed to
migrate
to the cities and steal the shit jobs

we're not supposed to
use
names like Charles or Harry or Grace

we're not supposed to
mock
the queen at Holyrood Palace

we're not supposed to
mock
the queen at Buckingham Palace

we're not supposed to
mock
the queen at Westminster Abbey

we're not supposed to
act
like we are above ourselves

we're not supposed to
remain
forever the lower orders

we're not supposed to
'live long and prosper'
as part of the infinite natural structure

we're not really supposed to
be here any longer
yet here, here we are

  —good night!

whose anonymous crimes are these?

who are you
who are you
tell me, please, who the fuck are you

did you die in 62
with shamrocks on your shoes
tell me, dæmon, who the fuck are you—

wise old woman
with thistles in her hair
gave us balloons to soar into the sky

dirty little man
with a spanner on his hip
left blind-innocence with a broken skull—

every trust was trampled the day you were born
jesus nor buddha could redemption bring
there was silence in the forest, filthy shadows on
    the streets
winter storms in radioactive zoos

be much better if you're dead
no more seedlings running red
from your squalid hands and monster rendezvous—

turns out you were a bomb from America
from India, Pakistan, France, Russia, Israel
you were China, North Korea and Great Britain too
tell me, dæmon, who the fuck are you

who are you
who are you,
please don't flash me once again,
please don't show me dæmon

who

the

fuck

are

you?

dare into dark

dare
to be different

dare
to be yourself

let
no gloomy bastard

oppress you

*

and when you pray
to your king everlasting

when you're in his arms
he doesn't give a damn

each day you wait
while his ignorance accrues

of your every pretty dream
and want and need

*

you're acutely aware
of being acutely aware

and still he doesn't care
about your economic mess

how to earn a crust
from the writing of yarns

and still you go on
alcoholic re-reformed

filling up your time
with sugar-cake and rhymes

say boo
to every evil in your twisted soul
and say goodbye
goodbye, goodbye

to all that
and all that's left as well

*

ideology
from the outside in

all a human construct
all a human construct

animal really
in its heart

*

and how do your eyes work
and what do you perceive

what can travel through
your iris densely-dark

little light vibrations
that tremble in your heart

in your heart
in your heart

waiting for a small war
to escalate and boom

send you to your tomb
where you'll sleep it off

sleep it all off
in his everlasting non-existent

king-like
bloody arms

a street near you
(or, 'pessimism of the intellect, optimism of the heart')

...you don't know
where you are
who you are
what you are
or what you have time for

a never ending cycle of ceaseless debt
a meaningless treadmill of dullard regret
holes in your shoes and your phone is broken
indignity grasping like a noose round your neck

catch your breath
let the city stretch and sweat
take your time
consider the maps of all the mountains you have
    climbed

breathe easy, gravity won't fail you
so don't push that chair away

look upon that unmapped city they call morning

awaken into infinite surprise
and rub the sleep from doubtful eyes

catch your heart
let love grow amidst the flowers of rage
catch your smiles
consider the brightness of your longest summer
    days

it's the horror and the beauty of a worker's song
a body may be weak when the mind is strong
yeah though you are tired and destitute
if the devil's in the details you can rewrite the book

rise up, you know who you are
stand together, be proud of who you are
be the sisters and the brothers
of the human revolution coming soon,
to street near you, coming soon...

sputnik
    music
        box

    soaring into nowhere

    on the mantelpiece

    the modern
      world
  beneath our feet
     and fear
of Russian invasion
before we grow old,
of revolutions bought and sold,
of the value of history
as trinkets and baubles,
      faithfully,
        rolled up in Friday's
fish n chip newspaper
     before the Chinese
arrived with take-aways,
     two-systems, clay-men
     guardians of empires—

Laika The Dog's
    exploding heart
      brought little thought
  of animal rights
neither moon nor pizza meeting her eyes
    but died in terror, shock and surprise
while humans
    took their tea before bed,
       supper, the tv

closed as a fading white dot and
when they've gone to sleep with the queen again,
    we wind the sputnik music box, it chimes
The Internationale
    unites the human race,
        in our slumber
        and in our Scottish corned-beef heads
tomorrow
    the QE2 will slip from its chains
    as yesterday's yesterday slips down the drain,
time will slip away again, and again, and again,
           time, time, time, time
              always slipping away

Hungarian Tractor Song

was very long with too slow a beat
for our neat 1960s heads
the plastic model of the Hungarian Tractor

so much better than a Lego one
but
manufactured behind an iron curtain—

we donned our woolly balaclavas
balanced books upon our heads
to keep the radiation at bay

we went out to the garden hut
with a tin of Heinz beans
to survive the shock wave

we cut our brains out
not to think about strike first
and mutually assured destruction insurance

the bomb, the bomb, the bomb,
we cried,
how can America sleep at night

when they have more nukes
than the rest of the planet
put together, it's all

one universe,
and the plastic Hungarian tractor
looking nothing like dull agriculture

is shiny, just like the bomb,
and other nightmares
most mundane

all your bitters sweet

all your stars
shot down
the screen goes blank
the mind's astray,
days gone away

Vinny and me,
our dads were cinema projectionists
in smoky rooms
the spectre of cancer
bit into the backs
of their lungs

they won't be back,
the job of projectionist
now defunct, life
nasty
brutish and short, maybe,

but
joyous
sublime
and
amazing

days   still   shine

1969 ?

(for my brother)

ah mind
aboot 1969
ma brother
goata album
tae stick stamps in,
generally unfranked,
country by country

mibbe wur auld communist
grandfaither
gave um it
coz thir wizza lotta
stamps frae
Hungary, Poland, Russia
Czechoslovakia

mibbe oor ither
grandfaither
the not communist
grandfaither
gave um
stamps frae
the USA, Australia, Canada, South Africa

like the Cold War
wiz gettin played oot
in a thirteen year auld bohys
cooncil
         hoose
bedroom
         in Borrheid.

breakfast – a sequence about myself

breakfast 1966

i forgot all about
the world cup,
the coal man
climbing
back bent steps
ragman's bugle
soot
sails from chimneys
ships slip into
the cold dark river
sleek and luxurious
not for the likes of us
a little puff of smoke
from Harold Wilson's pipe
white heat technology
formica-topped tables
magicole lights
and blazing red bars
on the new electric fire
black n white batman
impossibly falling
from a three wheeler,
tricycle, bicycles
too big
for the likes of us
industrial weans
born out of wedlock
but pretending to be in
some church or other

all the same
cornflakes
gravy scarcely remains
an option

breakfast 1976

waken
to the warmth of morning
brand new
bright sun of the heart
delicious
breakfast of infinite light
travelling
on through space and time
familiar
voices always loved
—get up, I won't tell you again
crystalline
frost inside the window
magical
chill of shivering winter
before
the porridge

punk rock foetus
skids and skirls
through
a bag-pipe womb

breakfast 1986

25 years old
and Scotland
still haven't
won the world cup,
head a mess of epilepsy
been through
several jobs:
milk boy
store boy
student-chemist
drummer
community worker
civil servant...

...have a bright idea
on the Causeyside
'I'm gonny be a writer'
and Helen asks
'What will you write?'
'Stories, poems aw that shite,
everything I possibly can, I'll type.'
lucky for me auld Tom Leonard
and his beard and his hat
were aw in town that day...

...and somewhere doon the Glasgow Road
Graham Fulton and Bobby Christie
separately had the same idea
we found each other and more folk too
the stuff began to flow...

the industrial present
crashed around us

shipyards sank
factories melted
making us
truly post-modern
in a wilderness
of market-forces
of private good and public bad
assets stripped
communities robbed
loadsa money
City spivs
with phones
the size of bricks
done deals
pulled tricks
and left us haunted, homeless
fucked and fucked-up
lunatics,
the addicted,
all had individual personal problems, of course

it was never their intention to steal everything,
they emptied the asylums, it was never
the free market that did anything like that,
like fuck it wasn't,
and
breakfast was
a teaspoonful of peanut butter
topped off with a raisin

breakfast 1996

little money
cozy corner flat
in glorious
Govanhill
Irish bars
and Queens Park
felt like time
for me to be
a father
fickle fate
took a bitter twist
and nothing
came of that

sadly sunk
into
walking
and drinking mad as fuck
ruined
ended up at a counsellor's door
John boring Major
was sinking like a boulder
it was cold inside his tent
but outside it was colder

forever
marching through the mud
Sisyphus eternal
pushed on up that hill
often there's a price
added onto your mistakes
I thought a great deal
of Tannahill's songs,

of his watery suicide day,
but closed my eyes
and carried on living
let time flow its own way
the personal is political
in a daze of marijuana
most mornings
I just munched a lot
of muesli and bananas

breakfast 2006

it was
Brilliant summer
and
everything to love

Brown and Blair
put an end to
'boom n bust'
their public spending
somehow reached me
I was back in Glasgow
for a PhD, academia
was a very peculiar place to be
after five years painful exile in Edinburgh
- penance for some real
or imagined sin,
where I got a little acting in

Dewar's parliament had popped up already
- as a preservation tactic for the Union,

homelessness appeared to disappear
far fewer beggars on the street
a cheering sight to see, not see
sleeping bodies huddled in doorways,
I was busy writing,
reading history,
reading everything,
and had a fleeting appearance on TV
released from poverty's grinding stones
—at last—
though life remained
what the middle classes
might call precarious,
but I didn't care
cause for a few year
my little income
would be guaranteed
what luxury not to have to count
the cost of every single tiny item out

the only thing to do here
was get busy
let my damaged mind heal
in its rotten auld core,
mornings
routines
walks
and little choices
unformidable

at breakfast time
I worked on a novel
that I'd later call
Punk Fiddle

breakfast 2016

leave god to the gods,
among people let all rights be equal

back in the 1780s
Thomas Paine
explained
democracy, citizen's rights, the social wage
but in 2016
many still cling
to aristocracy
private property
greed
and their auld Irish friend Edmund Burke —

back in the same
auld skint street
money tight
relentless writing
never give in
always saying
never give in
til everything's done:
the face of the planet
no longer graced
by the present

keep eating the porridge

a wee bit tutoring
creative writing
and other people
to help keep ye cheerful
as death walks on ever closer—
                              chin up son

Birthday
(by Alvaro de Campos)
Fernando Pessoa
(from the English of J.Coston & T.Leão)

Back in the day at ma birthday pairty
Ah wiz cheery an naebdy wiz deid.
In yonder auld hoose, ma birthday,
it wiz even centuries aulder than me.
Oor joy, your joy, n ma joy, wuzziz good iz
    any religion.

Back in the day at ma birthday
Ah wiz that fuhlla joy, ah wiz daft.
Ah cared nuthin fur hopes headin furrit,
Wiz the brains o oor hail clan.
Later, whin hope ah wiz needin, ah didny ken
    how tae hope,
An ah just couldny fun any meanin, as lang
    at ma life ah did peer.

Fur ivrihin ah thoat that ah wiz,
Fur aw in the heart an the hame...

Whit did ah tak frae oor cosy nights
Frae being loved and secure as a wean?
Whit? oh my God, an right just thismorn ah
    kent,
Noo it's gone, aw loast, canny funnit,
It's aw gone so faur away.

Back in the day at ma birthday
Whin ah wizny cauld, damp an auld,

An there wiz nae mould oan the wa's.
The day am the mould in the hallway,
Am a hoose o tremblin an tears,
The hoose o ma loved yins is sold,
Ma loved yins aw deid,
An me bae maself, just a spent match heid,
   just a skelf ...

Back in the day at ma birthday,
Ma love, we are livin *this* time,

Oor souls an oor boadies will meet there again,
For houghmagandie, plus, the divine.
Lovin masel like maself loves you,
We'll wolf doon the past like butter an breid
Nae time fur worries tae trouble oor teeth,
Ah see it again razor sharp, but am blin tae aw
   that's right here;
The table is set furra throng, wae glasses and
   china sae fine,
Sideboard loaded wae sweeties an fruit, an mer
   sits just oota sicht,
Auld aunties and cousins aw come frae afar, an
   aw because o me.

Back in the day at ma birthday...
Stoap, my heart's gonny brek, I canny think...
Uch, leave thinkin just tae the heid,
Uch God, dear God, oh my God!
Ah canny be arsed wae ma birthday,
Dinnae pairty fur thon anymer,
Ah just coont the days,
An ah go oan ma way
An ah'll be auld whin am auld.
That's it.

An am fashed wae masel fur no haudin,
The jewels o the past in ma pouch,
Back in the day...
Whin they
        celebrated
ma birthday.

Weird Pleasure
(A death of rationalism)

The sun cast long weak shadows as it roused itself. Everything appeared in a state of weird pleasure. Her porridge tasted better than ever. The mail was all good news. The troubled breathing that made it difficult taking the stairs had vanished. The melody of birdsong was gentle and tuneful. Sounds from cars and other oil-based vehicles had ceased to be. No one was rushing anywhere. She was really listening for the first time to a new vibrancy of everything. All perceived and yet to be perceived occurrences and situations had arisen and apprehension was effortless. Of course she was dead, it was inevitable from the.

>   listening so still
>   lush leafed trees
>   branches reaching out
>   inside your soul
>
>   very very gently
>   entering your mind
>   forensic fingers
>   absorbing your thoughts
>
>   they feel
>   that you are mad
>   or
>   mentally exhausted
>   or just
>   pure mental

aye

Who the fuck baked the tarts?
The English, The English baked the
   tarts!

Are you still in love with yourself
With yourself
With your beautiful self?

And who buried Karl Marx?
The English, The English,
The English buried Karl Marx

aye

It's the boy next door
He's driving you crazy

WHO THE FUCK SAVED THE QUEEN?

The girl upstairs
With the really loud daises

WHO THE FUCK SAVED THE QUEEN?

The Germans, The Germans
The Germans saved the queen

WHO THE FUCK SAVED THE WORLD?

USA, USA
Trump saved the world today
aye .. eh ..

Everything appeared in the State of
Weird Pleasure.
His porridge tasted better than ever.

if i was Pablo Picasso
(or The Porridge Song)

if i was Pablo Picasso
i'd be smaller and balder and Spanish
but turns oot i'm taller and Scottish
cause huge bowls of porridge i eat

i have porridge at dawn for my breakfast
i have porridge soufflé for my teas
and after a good porridge curry
i go for long runs on my knobbly auld knees

if i was Pablo Picasso
i'd have porridge tae the end of my days
i would be not lonely or sad
and i'd smile as i go on my way

but i am not Pablo Picasso
i'm just some auld dude farting words
i have nothing to say that is royal:
can't wait to be dancing in mud.

                    or burnt to a crisp in a box.

Kafka's Shorts

Gregor Samsa

life too hard

no passion
for struggle

life too hard

retreat unto death

A President of the Republic

The aMERICAN President Trump
is a merciless shade of orange

making him still more Scaddish
than the origins of his mere mother—

under Constitutional strain
bullet holes appear in Polling Stations

as ever expanding abysmal catacombs—
new hide-outs

for that gang formerly known as
The Hole in the Wall Gang—

of course, his Vater spake a wee bit German
not unlike myself and that other dead nut
Chuck Buk

Whistle

he was awakened by a whistling in his lungs
it was perhaps a response to the whistling of
   populist politicians

or was it something more deep-seated—
there were no appointments available with any
   clinicians

he convinced himself it had arisen from an
   injury to the upper torso,
the time when his father had bombarded him
   with cooking apples

when he was a child

Un-Spared

father died when he was young

and in so doing
did not use

his legs, feet, or shoes
quite as much

as he might have done

his pension contributions too
appeared to disappear

Live

there is a 'they'

and 'they' do not let us
have enough to live

very well
which is why our lives are short

we think we know who 'they' are
but we do not

and there are conspiracies everywhere
if it wasn't quite so Kafkaesque it would be
Orwellian

Lurking

aware of it or not
paranoia is always there

there is an epidemic of crime
of which the public are constantly reminded

this to make sure
the paranoia never completely

disappears from our minds

this is to make sure
that we can never trust

anyone else

not even our own children
who call for our heads

Drifters

Karl Rossmann was busy
but somehow drifted into the orbit

of The Oklahoma State Circus
which in the end

turned out to be
another dead end

Robinson and Delmarche
could not save themselves

despite their cunning
they could not see the sky above them

Rossmann had slipped through their fingers
and Robinson and Delmarche

remained merry in their squalor—
addicts of the short-lived modern day

Confirmation Scuttle

the old coal-scuttle
had been economically

redundant for decades—
both the result of

and resulting in
a toxic bleak environment—

but this was where the young family
found they had to make their home

Mister and Missus Jones
who were not legally married

had chosen that title for the sake of their children
Jesus, Mary and Joseph

they had to have some kind of myth—
something unreal beyond themselves to cling to

Eclipse

the permanent eclipse
meant cold and dark forever

such a deathly metaphor
'the permanent eclipse'

movement

finger twitching
time of life

's beautiful
dirty world

we come
to die in

*

don't sit
n wait

get in
aboot it

make a move

*

last time
ah saw yi
fuckin great
jist fuckin great

that's aw

*

it's just that i love you so much
i don't want you to leave me

it's the empty air where you used to be
that makes grief so unbreathable

*

destructive elements
in an age without trust

in hunger and thirst
there is lust

some lodged their faith
in mass extinctions
in despicable A-bombs

as we watched in disgust

*

where are your big guns
inescapable threats

from a center-right front
it's nothing we won't

all die to regret

*

imagine we're out
on the march and on strike

god idles and mocks
thinks to decide

to just laugh with disdain
or to shoot us on sight

or just steal the vision
send it back hollow

once it's put in a story
and then put in a book

with geeks of mistrust
who don't care how they look

at mistrust on mistrust on mistrust

dust and ashes, but

your mortality is my mortality
our being is all we have,
no like twa dugs warm by the fire
well-fed, healthy and secure,
while the outside world is dire

your blue moon is my blue moon
if we've still eyes to see,
rocks are thrown and meteors fall
one willed the other free,
outside, folk are running, others crawl

your humanity is my humanity
the earth our sacred source,
a major rainbow came our way
a joyful slide or hill to climb,
and guide to navigate all troubled days

your strong arms are my strong arms
I'm a drowning man who's walking,
your love withdrawn and I am gone
an artist pissing snow,
red eyes sunk below the sun-blood dawn

your river is my river
the living stream flows onward,
brainstorm-tears and earth-worn time
skin-cracked scabs of rage and sad,
this fragile mind that's mine

your body is my body
irreligious and unholy,
a family outwith convention

working for things human and humane,
before our bodies fail
in history's retribution and redemption

And your memory is my memory,
and I remember Graham and Tom
and I remember Davy and Rab
and I remember Roy and James
and I remember Janet and Johnno
and I remember Russell and Rita
and I remember Betty and Joan
I remember days, all full, when water tasted so
    much sweeter

song of worry and darkness

worry and darkness fill your heart
friends and lovers disappearing everyday
dark so thick the heart dissolves inside it
watch you try to smile through unsmiling lips
people doing their best to get through the day
but our health is poor with poverty and rage

i hold your hands in mine to find the echo of
    your heart
bring bread and fruit and tea to try and make
    you strong,
winter here is so unfair on those who cannot
    heat their homes,
priests and doctors useless, while politicians
    look the other way

quiet deprivation creeps inside our homes
impossible decisions made by millions all alone
who knows who will come or go or stay
refugees to accident, alcohol and valium
there is no net to catch you when you fall
i hold your hands and listen for your breath

wait for the revolution of your soul
a million ancestors turning in their graves

weary fragments, weary songs

the certainties of 1969
were the same uncertainties as now

blind faith in free markets
and all too human frailty

made for the greediest bastards
making off with all the money—

hangovers of war and slavery—
and new wars and new slaveries

to be pursued with the gusto
of rocket ships and atomic bombs

no wisdom,
merely weary fragments

written 'not
for the hopeful young'

*

...I
mean,
they're the royals after all

they shouldn't have to fly
amongst the riff-raff

or eat with plastic cutlery

or brush their own teeth

or change their bedsheets
or clean their own damned toilets

OMG
listen to me chuntering on...

*

this would be our wisdom not—
in streets for shelters we did rot
our human hearts too frail to sigh
though young, we die
beneath the loving arms of open sky

*

idiotic
smiling
men in suits
forced
us at gunpoint
—the never funpoint—
to leap from the bridge
unfurling civil war
they shot our own

OMG
listen to me chuntering on...

*

weary wae life
and weary wae worlds
the sun never come to lift our hearts
and off to war they made us march

the fools

*

china knows
that we mean business

they'll make a deal
with us now

*

we loved the warming summer sun
for the winter damp so hurt our lungs
and stupid cars with grime and fumes
were little help for breathless girls and boys

*

Awake! All hail, awake and sigh
no money's ours and we must die, too young—

weary wae life
tired o the world

what bloody minds this hell unfurled

74

*

I'll keep ye hale n hearty noo,
sing no oor departing song—
recall these street where once we walked
where tears noo blind oor een—

for weary is oor life
and weary is oor world

song of the deep-fried dug

i'm so hungry
i'm so hungry
i'm so hungry
i'm so hungry i could eat a deep-fried dug
     (deep-fried dug)

it's my west of Scotland working-class poverty
    narrative
and i hope that you won't think me too pejorative
when i say:

those West of Scotland toffs are much too greedy
with their brats in private schools they're oh so
    needy,
while our weans love white bread and food-bank
    beans
—our obese, diabetic, future does not gleam

i'm so hungry
i'm so hungry
i'm so hungry
i'm so hungry i could eat a deep-fried dug
    (deep-fried dug)

The
Renfrew
Road

prologue

yes   it may
or may it not

be after four

and there may be
no sunrise

anymore

five lives in one

there's my real life
and my dream life
and other lives
all intertwined

but i don't like
yet i do like

when it all
gets mixed up

inside

i am a profound
merchant banker

i am woman
i am man

i'm beyond all plans
of humans, of gods

and of alien dreams
i don't quite understand

i love the pink pound
i love excess unbound

get wide with me
i'll pummel and shaft

your little working-class arse

til pained and broken you'll scream

oh little bunny... scream!

—

there's my old friend Dan
he's a very dead man
he's a clansman wha died at glencoe
he a native ameri-can
can do kin kinda man
he's a ghost wha can travel in time

—

there's my new friend Diane
she's a girls' kinda man
she can go in the clubs
all night long, she can dance
she can sing, do astronomy too
can right run riot right thru Theresa's Cunt

And Theresa's Cunt is the best night club

any body   ever   ever   knew

has landing strip   has helicopter pad

has a needle that points to the north
just in case some poor migrant gets lost

—

travelling light
just passport

and toothbrush
we don't stop

for respite

the toothbrush
can open

all
borders,
fences,
people
and doors

while the passport
keeps everything

all
bright,
white
and clean
live your dream, live your dream, live your d r e
a m-mmmmmmm

—

Danny long-hair
ghosts along the road

a diabetic man
with a vision

and a plan
for the future

a street guru
on a brand new day

with battered guitar
and something to say

about dreaming revolution
and a Scotland that's free

of the dirty old hands
of the aristocracy

and the british royal family on the bbc
thrice nightly

at least
we all know our places

let's dream our way free
from the ugly faces

of our careless rulers
and their white-washed history

while a swarm of academics
sell us british history

as the dreams of our rulers
who were all enchanting and charming

and could never break a law
because all the rules they had approved

—

and the Renfrew Road is long
and common life is shorter

than expectation
would suggest

work and want and corporate
man-u-fact-urers

steal seconds of our breath
every second from our caves

and their fashion sense
much outshines our own

—

Miss Diane
she has frocks

that will blast off your socks
and she'll suck those bent cocks

any old time—
she snort high grade cocaine

out the window
from a thimble in the rain

she can massage the stars
she can take you to Mars

and all other destinations un-named
cause it's one law for her

while the rest sit oppressed
naked beneath blankets in prisons

with their little tiny coughs
with the cuffs on or off

little choice but what the guards give and
take—

Diane she can dance
she can rant rave and trance

morning papers to wrap the poor dead
paupers
serve them up on the pier

serve them straight, monk or queer
serves them right for being very very poor

serves them all right,
all those worthless little whores

the doors to their dreams are all closed
now

Harry Haller he don't dance here no more
he barred from Theresa's Cunt

for a fashion offence
and being a curious man—

poor Harry, poor Harry, poor Hermann

trees

there's pop
and there's rock

there's the private sector too
it's the glue holding all strands together

there's wood to burn
and there is access to guns

and rockets that can pin-point the dead

we can scurry and climb
sit aloft all sublime

with our feet on the decks
of our loving old oligarchs' yachts

we have branches
we have networks
we have a mentality
that rains down like leaves in your mind

we know your devices
we know where you've been
what you like, what you hate
what you've seen

no one's spying on you
that's a paranoid view

and you have only one body
to live your life through

we know who you are, we know what you do
we know exactly when you're going to die

—

Canadian something
tree with a massive trunk
see it on your tube
you know you've been there
with no one watching

red wood
dead wood
hard wood cock
word association
all comes back
sexual needs
we can exploit

prise from
your grubby dumb hands
every little penny
that you ever held dear
give us it

give us it in plain sight
thers's nothing of the night about us
for us your time does not exist
because your money
because your love
because your state of mind
has ceased to be your own
all of it, all of it, is ours alone

—

think yure an Inuit
think yure an ice-hugger
think yure melting underneath an over-ripe sun
there's a layer of plastic scum floating on the sea
and there's nowhere for carbon
there just aren't enough trees

think yure corned beef
think yure palm oil
think yure unrelenting desire for ancient timber
shiver shiver cold outside as you're fleeing from
    the sun
in the north you're most unwelcome
they want you all right back from where you've
    come

you can live in a tree-house
live a free life free from doubt
little insects crawling round you
not a problem in the north
you can squirt them dead
with chemical sprays and guns
what fun!

—

huge green arms
wave at puny humans

waiting for the two-legged monsters
to stride forward in their damned-apocalypse style
they think it is something
to chip away a little bark

with letters from their
higher level of reason

their alpha-betti-spaghetti
or their chain-saw massacres

that help no one at all
perhaps it's only they who glide to suicide

childish drugs

off our heads
with reproduction
and the new asexual
brand of twenty-four-hour
machine-sex

like those old games
we used to play
President Evil
and
Hunt the Cunt
shooting them down
getting reward points
to spend at *Shemazing Online Everything*
brand or no brand
lawless liberty

it's that thing
we used to do in Spring
sneak under the rafters
beams of sunlight
reveal spider traces
as we move
through an attic dreamworld
of newborn maps and stories
dreams translucent all-sex   never money
money was just for the old
and we had none anyway
— we had none anyway

20 billion
almost human

stalking the planet
mass extinction everywhere
and still we fuck and fight
murder street illegals day and night
but we are infectious
breeders
smothering tight
every natural surface
it's possible for us to cover

we are the all and everything of planet-e

history lessons

when William Wallace fell off his horse
the monks of Paisley Abbey of course
did not rush to help a lowly horse thief

no matter that he was a good thief
on the right side of jesus
on the right side like a Scottish Robin Hood

the birds sang in the trees
their words the weight of light
while humanity stuffed its ears to dull the tune

under the gaze of god the father
under the guidance of jesus the son
deluded monotheists all for one
Diane she lifted her fingers
and Dan he twinkled his toes
as from rough pasture Wallace the bold arose

chanting: freedom, freedom, freedom
for all, for liberty i'll answer the call
drink whisky until the day of doom

hark now boys the thistle's in bloom
arise from your hunger arise
and delirious enter the tomb

with conscience clear
and clouds overhead
quartered in your gory bed

with warm heart beating red
tossed aloft to feed the dogs
what are we doing here?

nothing but food for the trees
vessels for shipping disease
a plague upon the house of mother earth

when someone snorted and laughed
piled the bodies up on the cart
and the donkey entered Jerusalem

proclaiming love and peace at last
peace and love at last
peace, dead peace, at last

peace at last

that's entertainment

by way of greek and roman amphitheatre
any space became an arena for laughter or war

humans holding no notion of what they are for
hacked at flesh with lethal swords

dreaming the blood was recompense
for the cruelty of their deeds and words

that no alternative, nothing new, sun
shone in the sky with a mocking light

but couldn't put anything right

drowned in a broth of metaphors
still no-one knew what they were for

dance to remember and dance to forget
tied to each body a single mind

ever pulled to pleasure sublime
escaping the roots of the earth

that were much too cruel to live with
—much too cruel to live with

the reverie in the stars our only comfort
celebrities wank on their own words

what good fortune!

laugh to remember and laugh to forget
the past and the future and every regret
out of our minds with mechanical sex
yearning to lose our *self* in joys unbound—

and filled with awe inspiring
ridiculousness William Wallace stood up

got back on his horse
and rode away

breeders

the road crumble and decayed
fewer people walked its way
corpses piled on off-ramps
wounded stragglers in transit camps

others elsewhere formed a mini-state—
called it Cotland and they tried to generate
                                    children
a nation of infants
who
knew not what to do
as many women died in childbirth
stupid men following their cocks
foraged for food

while others, enraged,
destroyed and desecrated
all works of art
offensive to their eyes
—

94

it was May
when the cygnets appeared

in alliance with the trees
they were talking revolution

to overthrow the old regime
of the squalid infectious humans

the older swans were unconvinced
of necessity for action

for left to themselves alone
humans were all bound for putrefaction

not so, said the cygnets
and the trees sadly agreed

as they had misplaced affections
for those damned and upright monkeys

they had loved the silly sounds
of human songs

and enjoyed their rotting corpses
bringing fly and migde and raptor

curtail relentless desert's
northward march

—

and **the Renfrew Road**
is a long road

but no one knows or cares
where it is

where it's going
or where it's been

soon everything
will be unseen by any living human eyes

no more who, no more where
and no more why

and the trees don't want to meet
their cacti cousins

no more accidental deaths
ghostbirds flying into glass

or minced up in them windmill's
bloody arms

no more plastic   no more reason
no more   naming of the seasons

no more time
no more mythic gods and sods

and no more proclamations
that rise above the wind

with ape-mammalian power
never again, ever, cometh the derangement of
the hour

or of glass, synthetic compounds
or devil-dogs bred merely for their looks

no more purple   no more ermine
no more condescending sermons

spurting wryly from religion's purple cock-head
warmly welcome the human and the dead

human and dead
all the one and same

all unreal and rational
all that is rational is unreal

that's the deal the floating
universe beyond our comprehension

made with itself

only fucking in the name of its very own survival
nothing that those paltry human minds could
    ever rival

even with elaborate dancing
and ever more pointless appeals

to collective innocence
contained within an unseen collective strength
of the very same universal essence, hence

cometh the war, cometh the hour
cometh the cygnet, cometh the tree
cometh the crazy-dancing-human-monkey-tree
we aren't all capitalists now
we aren't all Americans now
we aren't any thing at all now
once breeders, now bringers

of their own special darkness
that they called their own extinction
wave good-bye humanity
let's all wave humanity good-bye

forgetting atoms dance

how could we be
so naive, Kathy Acker said,
forgetting she was dead
already
Diane and Dan
were dressed to go
in to-to action in stereo
with Kathy a glowing orb
between cunt and cock
and much too dead to shock

Dan had donned
his Native American shaman attire
acquired back in '97
knowing it was the only
counter-cultural empire
worth emulation

his inspiration hailed
from the north
how had they survived
the European invasion
that rubbed about everything out

Diane wore a boiler
suit industrial
sexless faxshion
they scrambled
to The Mall—
it was shut
ring-fenced
due to the war
it was useless
to even try to enter
the edifice
didn't know what it was for
—a worldly wonderful pyramid
stuffed with rotten
consumer non-durables
protected by soldiers and guards

instead
they head
along to the morgue
which nestles
on the bank
of a dried river-bed
here there's
a queue
of desperate
sad faces
seeking
the corpses

of friends
acquaintances
lovers
family members
disappeared queers
grannies
automatons
things and people like that

others are
curious
tourists
out to gloat
at the fate
that had not yet
thrust itself
upon them

Diane whispered into Dan's deaf ear
I'm hoping you will fuck me here
Dan did not reply nor notice
just how nicely Diane smiled

she'd whispered into his dead-nerved ear
how could he be expected to hear
though he felt her breath
caress his auld jawbone

his cock stirred in his pants
and he thought he might
like to fuck Diane right here
right now

every woman was an object
in post-capitalist corporate
Renfrew Road
every man refused to understand

that if all women were objects
then all men were objects too

a spectrum of genders
but sex required no spectrum
merely objects, required objects
power
and
exploitation
and
murder
an infinite
appetite
for objects
all kinds
of objects
to use as fuck-toys
armies of landlords
fuck out the brains
of vulnerable
human monkeys
dancing round
their discount cards
singing
we are all objects too
we are all objects too

—

alcoholic necrosis
murdering souls
amphetamine bleeding gums
guns at the ready
here come the scum-jake-pensioner-kids

and scientists
study the juices
emitted by bacterial infection
of the limbs
and send them in
to outer-space
to fend for themselves
as offensive space weapons
waging war against
the universe itself

—

in a cellular world
of innerspace

introspection
is the only road to follow

—

are we that part of nature
only striving to destroy

with our misanthropic melancholy songs

self-obsessive suicidal cock-cunts
how could we be

how *could we be*
how could **we** be
so naive
Kathy Acker said, so beautifully
she understands
'blood and guts in high-school'
isn't really fiction
under guns

there's nothing new,
it seems,
over the sun

at
the
end
of
the
rain
bow — no one gonny rush in and save us

anywhere else
there is this
that
and
the
other

who is the other?

sitting still

now, this body — this body, now

that i occupy — with more ease and comfort

than once was the way —
                 runs on its own strength

to get through the day — but says much less
           than it used to want to say

by way of complaint, protest and such
and that awful sickness made me run
for the white of the bathroom
and the upsurge of puke
that no kind of book was ever going to fix

no weird learning to unlock the mind
just let the body do its thing
and spend time hoping
'the future will be different'

while courage comes to gaze,
look through the window
with its nose to the glass
and when it leaves there's a mark on the
     pane,
let ideas grow, courage come around again

and this will be the day
my body gets comfortable
in itself and with time—
its passing and its iceberg nature—

the past all under water and the future
piercing — bright,
reaching for one vast, open sky

grey sky, blue sky, pink sky, orange sky,
    yellow sky
a sky to stretch — my eager body over —
and across the rainbow
to get there and take it —
make it mine, my body

now — this body — this body now —
        alive

epilogue

—

sunsets so spectacular
forgetting atoms
dance
the nothing new

—

ansaphone poems

hello
is that you urizit that machine thing
ach fuck that
beep
phone me back

**

hello there
jist been up tae see ma grandpa
eez dayn that stan laurel thing again
ye kin alwiz tell
eez hudda few haufs
whinih diz that
anywey
hi wiz chattin away
fuhlla life
the auld fucker
amazin really
anywey
cheerio the noo.

**

we are calling
to inform you
about a new
government
heating initiative

**

gutta knock back
ye in
ye hear me
gutta knock back
n thull no serve mi
gonny you go doon
get uz a boattla whisky
n sum fags
they widny even geemi the fags
um awright tae
fucking bastards
gonny you go doon
ach is that that fuckin machine am tokin tae
canny believe they widny sell mi fags
i'm 62
think they know whut age ah um
how auld dae ye need tae be
tae buy fags anyway
a knock back eh
no hud wanna them fur years
no furra.

**

we are calling
to inform you
about a new
government
awareness initiative

we wish to let you know
that we are aware
that you are unaware

please be aware
that it is in all of our interests
to be aware

**

ahv loast ma keys
thir somewhere in the hoose
fuck knows where
I must've hud thum ir ah widny uv goat in
here

kin you nip doon n gehtus wan cut
how much dae ye think it might cost
a fiver? merr than a fiver?
ahl geeyi money furra bevy anaw

**

hello mister ferguson
this is Carla speaking from the Royal Bank
on Alexandra Parade
Just to let you know
that the claim that you put in has been
successful
and the cash has been credited to your
account

it is now available to you,
thank you very much,
bye.

**

hello

winter comes
a fearsome killer

through the aged
darkening day

youth is busy
with its snowballs

struggling old folk
hidden away

**

howyi doin there
ah heard ye wur back the other night
geeza phone whin ye get this...

oh right ahv goat a new mobile number
I canny remember whit it is
so ahl huvtae phone ye back later

awright, ahv goat a day aff the morra
hope tae seeyi furra pint
if yir up furrit

**

hello mister ferguson
this is Carla speaking from the Royal Bank
on Alexandra Parade

Just to let you know
that the claim that you put in has been
unsuccessful
and the funds recently deposited by us
into your account
have now been deducted from your account
we are sorry
for any inconvenience
bye.

**

do you need
replacement
windows and doors

do you need
prosthetic teeth or limbs
funeral insurance
electric wheelchair
enter our raffle
and receive a free
gift write right
ink pen
with synchronised nib

let me stress
we are not Microsoft, Google or Facebook
this is a genuine offer
please enter your offer code
at www dot scammers-un-limited dot com

**

hello --- aye
jist tae let yi know
Rab died
that's him
gone
eh --- aye

ah hudny heard frae um
fur aboot two year either
last message hi sent mi
hi wiz askin 'is Fergie still a wanker?'
that's you innit
well uryi
uryi still a wanker?
ah don't know
layter man --- layter
ahl be in touch wae the funeral details
cheerio

**

Jim Ferguson lives and writes in Glasgow. His research on Paisley poet Robert Tannahill (1774-1810) includes *A Weaver in Wartime*, *Tannahill and Irish Song*, and *Radicalism in the Work of Robert Tannahill*, which can be found online.

Jim's website: jimfergusonpoet.co.uk

Ferguson's other books include:

the art of catching a bus and other poems
(AK Press, Edinburgh 1994)

Punk Fiddle: a novel
(Whirlpool, Edinburgh 2012)

The pine-box jig involves no dancing
(Whirlpool, Edinburgh 2014)

For Eva: selected poems 1990-2016
(Famous Seamus, London 2017)

when feeling fully at home in the drifting living room of time: selected poems 1986-2017
(Famous Seamus, London/Brighton 2018)

Neither Oil nor Water: a novel
(Clochoderick Press, Paisley 2018)

Poor Wurld
(Speculative Books, 2020)

Some of these poems have appeared previously in Live Encounters, The Projectionist's Playground, Gutter Magazine, A Kist of Thistles, Bridges or Walls, Raums, Glasgow Justice / Just Is, The Renfrew Road (pamphlet), and on the cd More Than Quirky. Some have been broadcast on Sunny Govan Radio. Some others may have appeared in places I have forgotten.

A big thank you to all who have published my work in past.